Escape to the farmhouse

Escape to the Farmhouse

one story of surviving domestic violence

ITSMYTRUTH

XULON PRESS

Xulon Press
2301 Lucien Way #415
Maitland, FL 32751
407.339.4217
www.xulonpress.com

© 2022 by itsmytruth

All rights reserved solely by the author. The author guarantees all contents are original and do not infringe upon the legal rights of any other person or work. No part of this book may be reproduced in any form without the permission of the author.

Due to the changing nature of the Internet, if there are any web addresses, links, or URLs included in this manuscript, these may have been altered and may no longer be accessible. The views and opinions shared in this book belong solely to the author and do not necessarily reflect those of the publisher. The publisher therefore disclaims responsibility for the views or opinions expressed within the work.

Unless otherwise indicated, Scripture quotations taken from the King James Version (KJV)—*public domain.*

Paperback ISBN-13: 978-1-6628-4864-3

Table of Contents

Dedication ix
Preface xi
Introduction xiii
The Beginning… 1
Years of Pain 3
The Struggle 11
Finding the Light 17
Forgiveness, Faith, and Reconciliation 19
Fear – Faith 21
The Escape 23
Arriving at the Farmhouse 25
2020 29
Light the Path and Lead Me 33
Endnotes 35

Dedication

This book is written in memory of the most loving person I have ever known, my grandmother.

Preface

I have weathered this storm... and still have a voice.

We each have a voice and our story to tell. This is my truth.

The truth not only frees me, but can be a door to freedom for others to find the healing light of God's love.

I feel it is necessary to tell my story of surviving domestic abuse and violence to help bring healing and hope to others affected.

> Through the tender mercy of our God, whereby the dayspring from on high; both visited us, to give light to them that sit in darkness and in the shadow of death to guide our feet into the way of peace.
> Luke 1:78-79

Introduction

In the year 2020, the world was in chaos over the COVID-19 virus, a global pandemic. The United States was erupting in violence over social injustices, and nothing felt "normal" in our lives. As the months of quarantine lockdown continued, incidents of domestic violence increased. It is estimated that 10 million women in America are affected each year[1]; I am one of those women. As the weeks of isolation continued, I felt compelled to share my truth, in hopes that it can help others.

It is important that each voice and story is heard, and that we learn to listen and understand one another. Anger and hate are learned reactions! We can help heal the pain and violence by loving more in our hearts and homes. The problem of domestic violence and abuse has a devasting effect on the victims and their children for multiple generations.

> "Love begins by taking care of the closest ones, the ones at home."[2]
>
> Mother Theresa

Escape to the farmhouse

Children who witness and experience domestic violence and abuse are changed by the trauma they hear and see. The damage caused by violent words and actions cannot be calculated in numbers alone. The long-lasting effects of this violence and abusive behavior can be seen in millions of broken homes and damaged souls.

Where do you turn when the damage is too severe and there is no safe place where you can seek refuge?

Seek refuge in the arms and Word of God and His people.

The story of humanity has evolved through millennia, with women struggling to bring forth children and helping them survive to adulthood. The shared experiences of generations are passed through family that survives. Women have been suffering from on-going and pervasive domestic violence throughout history.

There are domestic violence laws found written and documented by the Hammurabi code, nearly 3800 years ago (1792-1750 BC). These are the first known written laws, best known for the "eye for an eye" law. In the code, the laws state: [3]

Introduction

209. If a man strike a free-born woman so that she lose her unborn child, he shall pay ten shekels for her loss.

210. If the woman die, his daughter shall be put to death.

211. If a woman of the free class lose her child by a blow, he shall pay five shekels in money.

212. If this woman die, he shall pay half a mina.

213. If he strike the maid-servant of a man, and she lose her child, he shall pay two shekels in money.

214. If this maid-servant die, he shall pay one-third of a mina.

The information in 2018 showed that twenty-five percent of female homicides are committed by husbands or boyfriends.[4] The domestic violence group, NCADV

– National Coalition Against Domestic Violence -- stated that on average, twenty people per minute experience domestic abuse and violence, one in fifteen children are exposed to violence, ninety percent are eyewitnesses, and one in four women reported experiencing domestic violence in their life.

Thanks to God, I survived.

The Beginning...

As a young child, our family moved away from my paternal relatives and the small town in which generations had lived, leaving behind all the love and comforts of family. Apartment life in a large city was a world away from farms and fields of small-town America. The sights, sounds, and smells were overwhelming, especially to a small child. Everything felt strange and foreign. I couldn't sleep because I had no idea why my world had turned upside down.

At school I experienced the hatred and violence of bullying. The kids made fun of how I talked, my hair, clothes, skin, and everything about me that was different from them. The bullying continued daily and became increasingly intense as days turned to weeks, and then months. I became shy, quiet, and stayed to myself when I could, but they would find me.

One day, the mean words and constant teasing turned physical when a group of kids cornered me on the playground. The next moment erupted in violence, and the physical pain of being hit and kicked from every direction, and the emotional pain of seeing the hatred in their eyes, was unforgettable. Next came a blur of pain and violence, the confusion of what was happening and why, and then it was over. Whatever remains of you after the experience is forever changed when you feel the hatred that people are capable of expressing through violence.

Emotional, mental, and physical trauma can be overcome through strength, understanding, and faith. Enduring the physical trauma of being beaten, assaulted, spit on, and left for dead is only part of the battle. The emotional pain, being possibly worse than the physical trauma, was unseen, and the real challenge was the struggle to overcome those emotional scars.

Childhood memories are strange in the sense that the feelings and emotions are what comes to mind, not necessarily the exact events. The loneliness and isolation of being painfully shy and uncomfortable in my own skin affects me to this day. Desperately wanting to be loved left my heart vulnerable to those who hurt me as they said they loved me.

Years of Pain

Anyone who has suffered, endured, and survived abuse knows that survival is not enough. What is truly important is that we can find a way to heal so that our pain is not passed on to the next generation. We learn how to treat each other, and ourselves, from our parents and families. However, millions of us grew up thinking something was wrong with us because our parents had unhealed pain and were broken in their interactions. Unfortunately, the pain they caused each other hurt their children the most.

> "The world breaks everyone, and afterwards, some are strong at the broken places."[5]
> Ernest Hemingway

Unless you experience the pain and shame of being a domestic violence victim, you cannot understand its effects: the shame of allowing another person to treat you with cruelty, hatred, violence, and especially, the isolation from all your family and friends who care about you. It is even more painful to admit the overwhelming circumstances: financial, physical, and emotional strains.

The fear and constant stress of living through daily abuse is paralyzing. You feel alone, scared, ashamed, and worst of all, trapped in a situation that seems desperate and impossible to overcome. If you survive, the physical pain can heal, but the emotional pain remains.

The abuse and violence does not happen right away for most victims. It is a gradual process of isolation, separation, humiliation, and control. This is usually after a period of happiness and everything is "too good to be true," and it is a manipulation that many fall prey to. The beginning is literally sunshine and roses, but as time passes, the sunshine fades into gray storms, and the roses wither, then are gone.

The abuser learns all the ways that you are vulnerable, and prey on that vulnerability. Furthermore, if you are searching for love and someone pretends to love you convincingly, it seems like love. When you trust someone enough to see all of your pain and heartache, they should protect that information, not use it to hurt you. There are people who will learn to earn your trust, extract your secrets, and get to your heart as a way of control.

For some, only after years of being together does the verbal and emotional abuse become physical. When you are unloved, having no self-esteem or self-worth, it leaves you vulnerable to domestic abuse and violence. The abuser uses your need for love as a weapon of power and control.

The longer you are abused, the more damaged you become. You are less likely to find the strength to fight the fear and survive the escape.

When the verbal and emotional abuse continue for years, your heart is broken, your spirit weakened, and the violence escalates anytime the abuser feels they are losing control and power over you. Be careful who you trust your heart to, because it could be the wrong person. The next years were filled with pain, grief, bruises, and heartache.

My only joy was my child. After I became a mother, I used to take drives and cry about how much I wanted to fix the pains in my heart. I needed to figure out how to like myself, and this process was the most painful, dredging up all the past in order to move forward.

Once children are involved, the abuser's control increases. Your fear of them hurting your children is the ultimate abuse.

Recounting my story may be startling for some, but the truth of the violence needs to be told.

One evening, I had found the strength to leave my abusive boyfriend. The constant verbal insults and emotional torment had taken its toll. Preparing to leave, there were angry words exchanged and out of nowhere, he came up behind me, grabbed my hair, and slammed my face into the countertop with all his might. My face was shattered, swollen, and bruised;. that was the beginning of the attack.

Fighting for my life, I made it out of the room, trying to reach a phone and call 911, or reach my keys to get away. He ripped my purse and phone away from me and the fight intensified. Why? Because I tried to call the cops for help. He was determined to permanently silence me by grabbing my throat and placing his hand over my mouth to stop me from screaming and breathing. His intent was to murder me. I had only seen that dark, empty, evil stare once before, when I was violently attacked by a man attempting a sexual assault years prior. That dark, evil, empty look in someone's eyes is unmistakable, coming from deep within their soul: they want you dead! I fought for my life until the police came to the door; they had been called by the neighbors.

> The Lord saved me with loving kindness from the wicked who oppress me, and from deadly enemies.
>
> Psalms 17

In moments of darkness and fear, know that if you trust in the Lord, you are not alone. Every experience is giving you information that you need to make life decisions. The trauma does not define you; it shows you how much strength you have when you survive it.

> God is my shield
> I cried out to the Lord and he heard me
> I laid my head down and slept
> I awakened for the Lord had
> sustained me
>
> Psalms 3:4-5

Days and weeks went by and the violence was never far away. At any moment, it would explode, and the constant intimidation that it brought was smothering and unbearable. The stress of what and when the next violence would occur was always there.

In bed, I should have been able to sleep peacefully; however, in the dark of night, suddenly I would be jarringly awakened, with him grabbing me by the throat, and his knees on my chest, trying to take my life. This became a nightly occurrence. I did not know when the next attack would come, but each time it became more violent and angrier than before.

Escape to the farmhouse

There was nowhere to escape, no one to help, and no financial way to leave. I was trapped, wondering what night would be the one my child witnessed my murder.

The danger of violence and fear touching my child was overwhelming. I moved through life doing what must be done, but not living, just surviving. The isolation and loneliness were debilitating, more-so than the physical beatings and attempts to kill me. I reached a moment when I wondered if it would better if he did kill me. However, I never stopped fighting. I lived for my child to have a mother.

The days went by and the abuse and violence was never far away. At any moment, it could explode, into angry words, or throwing things, physical threats, or violence.

To those who tried to silence my voice, take my breath, choke me, beat me, and put fear into me, I say:

I am still here! I am not silent!

Years of Pain

And for those whose voice was stolen:

We all matter. We all mean something to those who truly love us.

Emotional pain can have a horrible long-term effect on your life, leaving you sad and broken. My spirit had been beaten and mistreated. I worried that the damage was not repairable. Tears were the pain leaving the body, I hoped. I had a river of sadness that needed to be released. The pain was so strong that it had physical repercussions.

The Struggle

When I was weak and exhausted from carrying the burdens of this life, I knelt down to pray and let the pain of the past and present fall off my shoulders at the Lord's feet, releasing all the worry. Only then could I truly embrace the joys and love that I had been given from God.

I struggled since childhood to be loved, and continued to fight daily to discover how to love myself. Sitting and thinking about the journey and the thousands of decisions, fears, lessons, and pain that I have been through. This made me know, without a doubt, that God has a plan for each of us. With each laugh and smile, my faith grows. Children are the blessings and grace of the Lord here on Earth.

There is no greater love than that of a child for their parents and parents for their child, and we are all God's children.

Sacrificing control over everything in my life is more difficult than I ever could have anticipated. I have faced millions of fears to get to a place where I can even begin to put my emotions into words, let alone have these words make any kind of sense. Our sense of self is all that we can ever hope to change. There are many things that we have no control over, especially who are parents are, and what that will mean for each of us. Our parents shape our genes, what we look like, what we know as children about how to feel, what is "normal," and the expectations that accompany it. Their struggles as people and parents determine our fates as their children. The idea of "family" determines our direction, whether good or bad. If my parents didn't like themselves, how could I learn to like myself?

There are many times in our lives where we are tested. You choose to struggle through, push on, and find out how strong you are, or you let it crush your spirit and soul. Many who have been abused, beaten, threatened, have lived in the hell of our minds relive all the harsh words and horrible experiences. Yet, somehow, if you overcome and persevere, you are aware of the strength within yourself. Everyone has difficulties and hardships to overcome. Some start in childhood, some are afflicted by others, and some by life's harsh events. It is our responsibility to help each other through kindness and respect. We show this to those who our lives touch, especially our children.

It is our responsibility as parents to stop these cycles of abuse, and to be strong enough to conquer the fears that

The Struggle

hold us back from being better tomorrow than we are today. The love we show our children, friends, and family is all the legacy that we leave behind. All the "things" we have acquired mean nothing, but the love ripples through time, like a small stone thrown into a pond. We are nothing but a speck of dust in time, except for the love we leave behind.

It is difficult as human beings to look into ourselves, and at our lives, and see our faults, mistakes, and missteps. The lessons learned in our lives are often the result of immense pain and grief. There is an old saying that says, "nothing worthwhile is gained easily."[6] Knowledge of ourselves, and having the wisdom to be a better version of ourselves, is as difficult as acknowledging one's faults and taking responsibility for their life.

Being abused is horrible enough, but you begin to think it is your fault when it is actually the abuser's fault, not the victim's. No matter the justification from the abuser, it is always wrong. I was physically and mentally abused by my boyfriend for years. It started with manipulation and evolved into full-scale emotional warfare, trying to control with fear. Sadly, this is a familiar story for many women who wanted love, but received nothing but hatred and pain. No one deserves to be intentionally hurt by the one who said they would love you forever. The constant assault on my body, spirit, and heart caused indescribable sadness. A flood of tears is the simplest way to understand my constant pain.

Somehow, I must find forgiveness and try to understand, finding kindness and compassion when my pain is overwhelming. Self-hating depression, grief, and sadness are feelings that left me hopelessly lost in the dark, feeling unvalued and ashamed of falling victim to domestic abuse.

> Sorrow is better than laughter: for by the sadness of the countenance the heart is made better.
>
> Ecclesiastes 7:3

The Struggle

How do you know it is time to leave? Trust in the Lord's words.

Time

To everything there is a season, and a time to every purpose under the heavens:
A time to be born, and a time to die;
A time to plant, and a time to pluck up that which is planted;
A time to kill, and a time to heal;
A time to break down, and a time to build up;
A time to weep, and a time to laugh;
A time to mourn, and a time to dance;
A time to cast away stones, and a time to gather stones together;
A time to embrace, and a time to refrain from embracing;
A time to get, and a time to lose;
A time to keep, and a time to cast away;
A time to vend and a time to sew;
A time to keep silent and a time to speak;
A time to love and a time to hate;
A time of war and a time of peace;
(A time to escape the violence).

Ecclesiastes 3, 1-8

Finding the Light

There always seemed to me to be something missing or hollow, but I could never put it into words before now. I did not have a life filled with the love of the Lord and the faith of spirit that it brought. I had been sad and for most of life felt worthless and never good enough.

The only person who I felt close to, who understood and loved me in spite of all my flaws and mistakes, left this earth and it changed my life forever. In my horrible sadness and grief, I was led to the light of the Lord Jesus Christ.

I never imagined my life's path leading me to a church. The people I met restored my faith in life and my future. I cried millions of healing tears in the pews, being thankful every day that the Lord saved me! The first Sunday I only listened and I felt touched by the words, as if they were meant only for me. Each time I went back, there was something that touched my heart: a song, a Bible verse, a child's smile, or a mother's love. I had been so lost and sad that I couldn't enjoy life or the people in it.

I had gone through the motions for many years, functioning but not really living. I had tried covering up the sadness, but it never worked for long. I really needed a cure for self-loathing and self-sabotage. I lived decades of my life feeling this sense of self-doubt, never having self-confidence or a healthy sense of self-worth. I want to share the pain, joy, and lessons I have learned to increase the awareness that loving who you are is the key to happiness. Joy is found in acceptance and giving love to gather love.

If you want to help stop the cycle of abuse and violence, you have to go out of your way to make sure your voice is heard.

All our words are given to us by the Lord.

Forgiveness, Faith, and Reconciliation

There is a healing that faith can provide, which I thought would never come. The freedom in your heart when you forgive the wrongs of the people in the past is amazing. The millions of tears I have cried feel worthwhile when realizing that you are healing instead of hurting. I have thought hundreds of times in my life that I wish the pain would end. I have imagined many ways to end it, and could never complete it because I have faith that I am here on this Earth for a purpose. My pain, wounds, and healing can be a light for others who are in the dark.

Taking the first step to reconcile can be the hardest step you ever take. You risk rejection and bringing up past pains, and if you never try, you won't ever know. Reaching out is the most courageous act of kindness you can exhort to another person.

I reached out to my mother after nearly fourteen years of being estranged. She lived in a neighboring county, but we could not have been further apart. I chose to write her a letter for the sake of my own heart, and I didn't expect anything in return. It was difficult to admit that I was wrong, but it had to be done.

I have struggled for many years with feelings of loneliness and sadness when I thought of my mom, and wondered why she didn't love me. She always had loved me and it took one short handwritten letter to find out. We both struggle with self-esteem issues, and it came from our past. Happiness in yourself is the best cure-all for what ails you. Accepting others for who they are and not judging them frees you. Every person is unique and it is not for us to question the work of the Lord.

There is a comfort and happiness that I have never known before I found the love of Jesus Christ.

I sat crying in a pew on a fall Sunday afternoon over the loss of my grandmother, and I felt a wave of comfort come over me. Tears are healing, and I have shed millions in my short life. We each have many opportunities daily to bring love into others' lives or pass by in it. We are in a world of one.

Fear – Faith

Do not fear what is next; have faith that God will provide and give thanks for what you have.

Fear can paralyze you and keep you trapped. You have to believe that you can be free, and have the faith to push past the fear to move on.

Once I started speaking with my mother again, I told her the first part of an awful story, and she finished the story with a memory of what she went through. That is the moment I knew why I reached out. She had a little farmhouse on a property that was hours away, and she said you and your child have to get away.

The Escape

> "The most difficult thing is the decision to act. The rest is merely tenacity."[7]
> Amelia Earhart

Fleeing from my abuser before the violence killed me was my only choice.

I had no idea of the sacrifices that it would mean for my life. No friends, social anything, and no more anything I had ever known. It was one of the most difficult choices to leave everything and everyone I knew, but it was necessary to save my child and myself. In the days before the escape, all I could think about was not getting caught leaving. I had a couple of friends who I could trust to help me on the escape night.

One would keep the abuser in sight and call it off if he came home unexpectedly. I had to wait until the right night to have a small window of time to put anything I could into the car and get away unseen. In one hour's time, I got some clothes, the photo albums, all my child's belongings and toys, an old mattress, and a few other things into the vehicle, and drove into the darkness. Not knowing where we were headed, how long it would take, or anything about the place we were going. I was simply driving and praying in the dark that it would be okay.

Faith and courage was what it took to leave everything behind and go into the unknown. We drove for hours before my heart rate and blood pressure returned to normal, but this was only the start of the escape. The farther we drove, the more the miles grew between my abuser, but the fear that he would find us was constant.

The most violence occurs when an abuser loses their control over the victim, and many don't live through the escape or attempted escape. I knew this from a police officer who privately told me, "There is nothing a protective order can do if he is determined to kill you. Just leave and go as far away as you can, and don't look back."

There was nothing anyone else could do; I had to be the one to choose life or death.

Arriving at the Farmhouse

The wilderness and the solitary place will
rejoice and blossom as the rose.
(Isaiah 35) –

I prayed
    for strength for my weak hands and to firm my
feeble knees.

[4] – Say to them that are of a fearful heart
Be strong, fear not,
    God will come and save you.

[6] – and a highway shall be there and a way
the redeemed shall walk there.

[10] – and the ransomed me shall return with
songs and everlasting joy, and they shall
obtain joy and gladness, and sorrow shall
flee away.

I am still here for a purpose; what I have endured will help me on the road ahead. I have never stopped moving forward, even though sometimes it was very slow, and I was crawling on hands and knees.

I have literally climbed many mountains along this journey so far, and been lost in deep valleys. The road of life I am on is many times rocky and I am bloodied from the travel on it. I was not saved until I was thirty-three years old, the same age of Christ when He was crucified, and betrayed by those closest to Him. Nothing I faced in my journey could come close to the pain my Savior endured. My prayers for salvation were answered and I was delivered from my abuser. I saved my child from growing up thinking that that abuse was normal, and would never accept that behavior.

Finding a way through the pain I have experienced is a difficult and tear-filled journey. As a child, when you are rejected by a parent, then as an adult rejected by the other parent, it is hard not to wonder: What is wrong with me? Why? To help me understand the damage done to me, I want to end this generational pain.

Forgiving myself for the past and the many bad decisions I have made is proving to be hardest of all. Escaping into the night and going into the middle of nowhere was tough and scary, but as the days passed, it slowly improved.

Arriving at the Farmhouse

Those days were difficult, and yet, as time marches on, the difficulty changes, never going away entirely. Knowing that you should care for yourself, and doing that, are quite different.

Selflessness and the grit to survive are both necessary to come through the experience that has changed me forever. The knowledge of self and what you are capable of is helpful for the many obstacles that one will face through this life.

After months of being free from my abuser, I am feeling better, though not completely healed. God has granted me the comfort and healing of His love, and I can release the pain and sadness, and embrace my time and healing. Now it is time to dance and laugh. Small things happen that give me the opportunity to heal existing wounds. Even after all that I have suffered, I am still open; my heart remains open to love and laughter, but it also opens me up to more pain. Being open and vulnerable still seem better than closing myself off to everything, both good and bad. I cannot allow the abuser to win by stealing my love from those in my life. My love and light is Heaven-sent, and I know that I am.

Years have gone by since my escape into the unknown. I put as much as I could fit into a horse trailer in one hour, and we drove off into the night. The fear of being found out was overwhelming, and all I had was faith that I was making the right decision. In that hour, I had to sacrifice nearly everything and everyone who I had known in my life up to that moment. The only thought I had was for my child to have the chance to a happy life. My life was in danger every day, and as the violence and abuse became more intense, I had to choose life before he took mine. When the breath of life is being choked out of you, and they have a look of murder in their eyes, you have to fight to live or give it up. There is such a will to live and fight for my life to be able to care for my child. I have at times in the past made decisions that could have ended my life, yet I survived. My child is the reason that I am alive, and I have a responsibility that all parents understand.

2020

When I was born, the year 2020 seemed so futuristic and far away. As I sit now during this strange time of pandemic and self quarantine, I realize the future is here. I read about pandemics all throughout history classes, in novels, non-fiction, movies, and most recently, in my own family tree. Diseases throughout the history of humanity have left many lessons to be learned. Throughout our shared history with this planet, the whole of humanity has left both beauty and scars behind. It is not unlike the battle in each human to find the beauty in the scars life leaves on us. Each of us has a story to tell, and in sharing the good, the bad, and the ugly truth of it all can help the next.

How we each came into this world is a story that we share with our mothers, and so on throughout the generations, back to a time and place that we all began, in the womb. The bond we share with our children and the fierce need to protect them, to have them survive, is the same, no matter the country, language spoken, culture, or time. That remains unchanged.

There are many struggling through life because they never felt accepted and loved. The unfulfilled desire to be loved and accepted can leave you vunerable to those who could take advantage of you. The lives of the victims of abuse are forever altered because of the violent acts committed against them. There should no shame in speaking about domestic abuse and violence.

Whether we are surviving the worst of the natural world: storms, volcanos, typhoons, earthquakes, floods, and a global pandemic;
whether we live differently or have widely varied cultures;
whether we speak different languages, have different spiritual rituals and beliefs;
whether the color of our skin is lighter or darker; and regardless of what neighborhood we live in,
we are all fragile, equal human beings..

In times of crisis, the differences do not matter. There have been humanitarian struggles for thousands of years over this simple right: we are all equal. The difficulties we all face are the same: feed ourselves and our children; find a way to keep ourselves and our children safe; and try to provide a good life for ourselves and our children. There are no differences in surroundings, countries, or continents that can change these fundamental truths.

There are many stories in the Bible and other sacred texts from various religions that relate the works, difficulties, and glories in this world that God can help us to see and overcome. These stories help us relate to and understand that there will always be challenges, obstacles, and hardships in life. The way to face each day is to have the faith in God that kindness, respect, and love can change your future days. Days can be filled with joy and laughter when you understand the value of your love to your children.

Each of us makes our small, daily impact, and watches that impact grow. A world with more respect, kindness, and love is all worth that effort. Each person has worth and value no matter their race or gender: every voice matters!

Light the Path and Lead Me

Love, respect, and kindness can make some small dent in the horrible plague of domestic abuse. Please help my words bring comfort to those women hurt by violence, abuse, and the self-loathing that being abused causes.

The Lord has chosen me to bring light to the dark shadow of shame of domestic violence and abuse.

I will stop mourning the loss of the life that I could have had.

All my decisions have lead me to this place.

Using what I was given, and what is right, I can use it to help bless others.

> Though no one can go back and make a brand new start, anyone can start from now and make a brand new ending.[8]
> Carl Bard

There are times throughout our lives, upon reflecting, that we can see more clearly: birthdays, the death of a loved one, the birth of a child, and holidays, including world-altering events such as pandemics or natural disasters.

The human spirit is amazingly fragile, yet each of us has a resilient spiritual energy affecting the world and those around us. Our time in this world is very short; we have, at best, one hundred years. The effect we have is but a small thread in the fabric of time. Many have come and gone from this world, with most leaving only little traces. Passing along the knowledge of how to love ourselves and others, being kind to ourselves and others, and being respectful to ourselves and others, is of utmost importance.

Each of us carries within ourselves the love of God. We are blessed with the light of life, but what we choose to do and say affects change. We need more love, respect, and kindness for all mankind. That is the world of God... one of love.

> And now abides faith, hope, love, these three; but the greatest of these is love.
>
> 1 Corinthians 13:13

Endnotes

1. www.ncadv.org

2. Love begins by taking care of the closest ones - t... quote by Mother Teresa (meaningin.com)

3. 282 Laws of the Code of Hammurabi | Know-It-All (wordpress.com)

4. www.ncadv.org

5. Quote by Ernest Hemingway: "The world breaks everyone and afterward many ar..." (goodreads.com)

6. Nothing Worthwhile Is Easy Quotes: top 9 famous quotes about Nothing Worthwhile Is Easy (wisefamousquotes.com)

7. Quote by Amelia Earhart: "The most difficult thing is the decision to act..." (goodreads.com)

8. Though no one can go back and make a brand new start, anyone can start from now and make a brand new ending. - Carl Bard - Quotespedia.org

CPSIA information can be obtained
at www.ICGtesting.com
Printed in the USA
BVHW031440140622
639735BV00016B/1410